Tipster:

A Look at How 9/11 Happened

Hillary Nan Goldberg

ISBN: 1468118250
ISBN-13: 9781468118254
Library of Congress Control Number: 2012901788
CreateSpace, North Charleston, SC

For Jessica and Ryan

Contents

CHAPTER 1

Catharsis: My Story

Tipster: A Look at How 9/11 Happened, was almost entitled *The Acceptable Truth*. This book covers the limited information given to the public by former Central Intelligence Agency (CIA) chief, George Tenet at the 9/11 Hearings; the measured minutia given to us by the Federal Bureau of Investigation (FBI), and the National Security Agency (NSA); and the truth that I can subjectively write about in this book.

Even though General Michael Hayden told the media on CNN that my deceased father was a former Central Intelligence Agency operative, (something about which he himself would rather have turned over in his grave than admit), I am grateful for getting implicit permission by Hayden via the media to discuss how this disaster happened. I try to bring threads together from my past and present in order to weave a tapestry of how I was able to see what the authorities failed to see, and how I became the "Tipster." I want to tell all my critics that no member of my family is involved in counter-terrorism, despite my observation of an erratic driver in a parking lot in Delray Beach. The driver turned out to be Mohammed Atta, the main 9/11 hijacker. In my opinion, the failure of the FBI to apprehend Atta, and his associate, who was also in Delray Beach, was caused by the combined actions of our elected officials, the nature of our foreign policy in the Middle East, and our failed justice system.

I first started writing *Tipster: A Look at How 9/11 Happened*, as a catharsis for my feelings of powerlessness about not having been able to do more to prevent 9/11. Also, I wanted to demonstrate to any citizen who, by the power of observation, and then by contacting the proper authorities, can save lives as well.

No one was more surprised than I was by the television coverage of my endeavor to get the authorities to respond faster regarding one of the complaints that brought me to FBI headquarters in West Palm Beach, Florida, on the last week of August, 2001. I want to reassure everyone that I tried to do what I could to stop the reckless murder of thousands of innocent Americans on September 11, 2001. I want to explain to myself, the victims of 9/11, and all Americans, that I tried to prevent the evil that happened that day, and alleviate my own grief.

My life felt like a near failure, except for a years-old memory of another train rider on Tri-Rail. On that ride, a young, African-American woman was kind enough to call the police on my insistence, as we rode through the Ali-Baba community of Miami. I had noticed some overt, but unexplained hostility I caught in the on-lookers outside the train, and I wanted to report it. Two years after 9/11, I heard that tip had been followed up and had saved the Sears Tower in Chicago from another terrorist attack by Al Qaeda.

Holding the 9/11 Hearings was a long shot as far as explaining why thousands of civilians have lost their lives. Part of the problem is that responsibility for the madness of 9/11 is only directed abroad, and not domestically at the politicians in the United States. There are politicians who failed and continue to commit civil and human rights violations right here at home. I include as examples a malicious Statute of Limitations, a Media Freeze, and a deceitful foreign policy that lets this nation's enemies prosper. These domestic factors cannot be discounted where responsibility for 9/11 is concerned.

In writing this book, I hope that we can conclude together that complacency cannot be valued in open society. We must condemn political instigators that take advantage of our weaknesses so that we may spot potential terrorist activities brewing that they have initiated before damage happens.

I know that I have received some minor criticism in the media for not coming forward, even though I have been unofficially dubbed "The Tipster" on one or two television networks. Here is my story. These are the opinions which I believe helped me in identifying the dangers I encountered then and may encounter again. Even though I may generate interest for my story and beliefs, I would like to state at the outset, that I would in no way have wanted 9/11 to happen despite any attention, or profit that could be generated from this book. My only hope is that all victims of terror will be thanked for their unwanted sacrifices that strengthen democracy and freedom.

Unfortunately, not much could be said in the short blips that have been dedicated to my contributions to the prevention of both 9/11 and the possible destruction of the Sears Tower in Chicago. In general, the coverage actually makes me a little nervous, as I was an intern at the New York Philharmonic when conductor Zubin Mehta and his ex-wife Nancy, suffered through the Whitewater scandal, and I saw how easily bad coverage can ruin a life.

In this book I am going to explain how an employee of the international publicity department of the New York Philharmonic becomes, as George Tenet apologetically described me, "the only sane one amongst us." At the 9/11 Hearings, he also mentioned that I am a descendant of Canaanite royalty, as well as indicated that my mental health was the reason why the authorities ignored my warnings. His description was a humiliating experience.

I suppose that most people in the world would guess that being a descendant of Canaanite royalty would make for an easy life. Unfortunately, it is otherwise. Firstly, my family had to accept that we were born, raised, and were living outside Canaan (Israel), in the Diaspora, even though we had always considered ourselves American. The first time we visited Israel, I thought I was in a dream. We stayed at luxurious hotels, including the Presidential suite at the King David hotel, and

I met my Israeli extended family on my father's side, either whom I had never met, or hadn't seen in years. I had just celebrated my Bat Mitzvah in New York, and I was still spiritually uplifted. My father was heartened to see his relatives from whom he had been separated by Nazi Germany and the turbulent aftermath of World War II.

My mother just blossomed, on seeing the historical sites, especially the royal gravesites of those to whom we were connected. My mother's genome is very historical to Canaan-Israel, as she is a descendant of the (House of) Ephraim, the rulers of Canaan-Israel. Ephraim I, an early king of Canaan of our lineage, is buried in Israel. (Senator John McCain visited this site while a presidential candidate). Our connection to this lineage dates until my ancestor, a prince of Israel, was killed by Babylonian conqueror, Nebuchadnezzar. This conqueror killed approximately half of the royal family, and the other half became a part of his empire during a time when the population was primarily militarized.

The lineage lasted almost five thousand years, one of the longest royal lineages in history. The House of Ephraim is believed to have fallen in battle with the Syrians and the Egyptians at Megiddo, Israel. In fact, the royal name of Ephraim lasted for seventeen generations, until the tradition of naming the living after only deceased ancestors became the norm. Additionally, the father of Ephraim I, also named Ephraim, was the greatest of Canaanite warriors, and is buried in Egypt out of choice, as a testament to the struggle and subsequent victory of his people. From the exhibit I saw at The Metropolitan Museum of Art, I could see that Ephraim was buried in a manner showing that the nation was on the cusp of paganism and monotheism. His ascent to the throne was at a time when his nation was just beginning to embrace the new Judaism of Abraham. The acceptance of Judaism as the family's religion occurred after his younger daughter, Nechama, was forced into inbreeding with his younger son, Hofni (even though another boy was substituted) by the pagan Baal religionist. Nechama died in childbirth, and the pain of her loss spurred the family to rebel against the paganism not only of Egypt, but of Canaan itself. Ephraim had four children; Tzippora, Ephraim, Hofni, and Nechama. Tzippora, who was the oldest, did not take the throne because she was female. Hofni married a non-Canaanite, Jewish woman of Asian heritage. Their daughter is believed to be the Hofnea, who is mentioned in the Bible as being killed at a well by Jordanians. Ephraim I is noted to have instituted laws that liberated the Canaanite nation, especially from the practice of falling prostrate, which was common amongst the Israeli/Canaanite slaves in Egypt. This is mimicked during present-day Jewish religious services as the congregants stand instead of falling prostrate. However, and this should be mentioned, the population hesitated to give him religious significance because, not only did he not want it, but also the older Ephraim was known to have extracted justice from Egyptian task-masters by taking prisoners of war.

I have not confessed this before, but my mother carried a subconscious, but gripping fear, not quite only of Arab terror, but also of the anti-royal tendencies of Communism in general, and anti-Semitism in particular. My father was actually more enthusiastic about possibly moving to Israel than was my mother. We even spent time on my great-aunt's poor kibbutz near Ashkelon, Israel, where my father wanted to teach me the importance of anti-materialism and subsequent gratitude for what we did have, not only as Americans, but as individuals on the successful side of middle-class capitalism.

Herod, a king of Israel who is often reviled by Christians, was not from the House of Ephraim, and is not in our lineage. In fact, my more recent ancestor was killed in battle fighting pre-Christian Romans, and his surviving widow and two daughters were exiled to Germany via Rome, where one of the daughters married a trader who had already taken on the last name of Elfenbein, and I am a descendant of Canaanite royalty by my maternal grandfather, Samuel Elfenbein. Much excitement was generated recently when human bones found at the Church of the Holy Sepulcher near Jerusalem were DNA tested and found to be related to Ephraim (the House of Ephraim).

I was fortunate to see some Canaanite royal artifacts while I was a high-school intern at The Metropolitan Museum of Art. I encourage everyone to see the exhibit when it travels. I have had invaluable cultural experiences, which I highly recommend to anyone, especially if you want to find out the facts behind Canaanite/Israeli history. Even if you do not want to compare the history to biblical accounts, you will learn from the exhibit. Canaan has a very ancient and rich cultural and spiritual history, which I often believe, is the envy of many nations.

My father's history perhaps was not as royal but was just as worthy. He had a Britoid ancestor of Scottish extraction, named Benzion, who immigrated to Canaan. My father was also a descendant of Johann Goldberg, an assistant to J.S. Bach, who, my grandmother used to joke, was "his right hand man," and he was a composer himself. My father was fair in appearance, which assisted him in being promoted from being a domestic agent for the CIA, to someone on international assignment, for which his appearance and somewhat mixed genetic background was appropriate. The story of my father's life always inspires me because he was a child of the Holocaust, born in Leipzig, Germany, where his father had gone into hiding from the Gestapo, Hitler's police force. With his mother and older brother, my father immigrated to the United States when he was five years old. It was a lonely existence when my grandfather had escaped as a stateless person to a refugee "hotel" in Italy. My grandfather, Benzion Goldberg, immigrated to the United States two years later. Both sides of my grandparents' families had members who were killed at Auschwitz concentration camp in Poland.

My grandmother had to sell their beautiful house in Leipzig under duress, a time which she remembered with bitterness. Most of her young brothers and sisters were able to go to Israel, and are, understandably, very proud Israelis. My father's life inspires me because he started his life as a child of persecution, and he was able to return, with the help of his adoptive country, to make a difference against totalitarianism. He worked against Communism, and was able to help democracy be victorious in Europe.

In high-school, I was known as "Scot Goldberg's sister," because my brother was a star pupil, especially in math. Also, I was an overweight youngster, which, brought a lot of misery, and particularly bright, which also brought a considerable amount of jealousy from my peers. It wasn't an easy combination. Old Bethpage seemed like a pretty, charming town; filled with large, comfortable homes and loving families. But, there was a drawback. Some of the worst child predators that you could imagine lived there, and men in the neighborhood molested both my brother and me repeatedly.

It was for that reason that I completely panicked one cold October day when a deranged fan happened to break through security and pay a visit to the publicity department the New York Philharmonic when I was nineteen years old.

Hence, you can imagine my disappointment when I heard George Tenet at the 9/11 Hearings, being questioned as to why my tip about Mohammed Atta was not followed through. He blamed the heavy case-load of investigation of domestic crimes as the reason that the FBI and CIA had become distracted and overwhelmed.

CHAPTER 2

Behind the Scenes

WHILE I WAS WORKING as an intern in the publicity and international media relations office at the New York Philharmonic in 1986, the Whitewater scandal hit. The Clintons were brought to court regarding the honesty of their real estate dealings. Life completely changed for our office from a state of privilege to one of fear. It became apparent to me and to my supervisor, Neil Parker, that Zubin Mehta (the renowned Indian-born conductor), was taken in by Bill and Hillary Clintons' personal and political charisma. Nancy Mehta, Mehta's wife at that time, was especially eager to conduct business with them, as they had quite an astonishing track record. Francis Little, the head of our department, breezed in and out of his office, while negotiating with journalists.

One day, Little came into warn us that we should expect bad coverage related to Whitewater and that he was doing everything in his power to ameliorate the situation. Promoters of classical music are used to the playing of music and not the playing of politics. Parker felt that we should blame Mehta's ties to the Clintons on Nancy Mehta, since she had some "dubious achievements" in her past, including in real estate; but Little overruled it. My suggestion, a press conference, was also overruled, even though we continued to generate publicity for the orchestra and its musicians.

Working for the New York Philharmonic had been a dream of mine since I was ten years old, but three days after Hillary Clinton had named Mehta as an investor during the Whitewater hearings, I knew that I wanted to leave. People who seemed like stalkers were hanging around the concert hall. I felt we needed our own Secret Service. Some of those hanging around seemed anti-Semitic, which was so cruel because Mehta was a convert to Judaism. I felt that my safety was in jeopardy and did not want to risk my life, even to work at as beautiful a place such as Lincoln Center.

Later in the book I will describe an attack that surpassed even after scenarios were painted by the NSA. Needless to say, that event took its toll on the mental health of our whole department. The Media Freeze that followed amounted to an outright abuse of power, as well as a violation of our basic constitutional right to Freedom of Speech and Freedom of the Press. The Media Freeze, to my understanding, was requested by Hillary Clinton under the advice of her media strategist, James Carville.

Mehta was just another investor, but he had a "gray-man" (a combination of security and advisor), to press the Clintons to compensate him. If you recall, back in the 1980's, it was not by law that developers had to compensate buyers for properties that were never built, but some of them did compensate their buyers anyway. To the best of my knowledge, the Clintons decided not to compensate anyone else. My whole department was nearly fired by Mehta.

As you are probably aware, most other governments have direct ties to the media, and I did not think that the parties in question were aware that my department, and the vast majority of honest journalists in this country, do not have such ties. If we had political connections, we would have given all of our energy to ensure that Mehta was not victimized as our blessed concert hall was dragged through mud-slinging. The "gray-man" even accused me and my brief encounters with Watergate journalist Carl Bernstein, as the reason why Mehta was being associated with the Clintons in a negative fashion, and he dubbed the situation "Whitewatergate."

One day, Nancy Mehta walked into the front of the publicity office, saying that the office should be disbanded, and that she was going to hire Hill & Knowlton, (the best people in the public-relations business), to handle Mehta's publicity. Parker and I looked at each other with a surprised glance. Luckily, we were able to dissuade her from that opinion. We persuaded her that such a move would generate more bad coverage.

Soon after the scandal hit, the Clintons encouraged the hiring of a secretary named Geri Eisenberg. Despite being the same ethnicity and close in age, we did not get along. In retrospect, I don't think that Eisenberg could handle the pressure, as she snapped at me all the time. On a sad note, I bumped into her on a trip to Israel about eleven years later. Then, she told me that she left the Philharmonic only a few months after I did, that she was on psychiatric disability, and living in public housing. My assumption is that her disability stemmed from the attack that affected our whole department. Even though Eisenberg and I had our constant quibbles, I would not have wished what happened on her, or on anyone.

In our department, there was a marketing professional named Thayer Preece Woodcock, and a senior secretary named Sheila Marie Johns, as well as Playbill editor, Barry Edelson. Edelson was fortunate enough to be absent the day of the attack. In that fleeting meeting in Israel, Eisenberg told me that Thayer had spent a year in a hospital, and I had already known that Johns suffered from manic depression. Only recently, I called the federal office of the Occupational Safety and Health Administration just in case there was a public safety issue regarding the concert hall and all its occupants.

One day, I caught Johns crying into her mirror. She was so upset for the Mehtas that she could not control her tears. She said, "Just to see him go through this." I felt sorry for myself. I was very angry on their behalf, even though they were angry at everyone else. It was a situation that creative people do not deserve. They do not deserve to be manipulated for political purposes, and our department did not deserve to suffer.

Toward the end of my internship, I encountered the future President, George W. Bush. It was not uncommon to encounter all manner of famous people at the concert hall. I overheard that he was worried that Mehta might play at the Democratic National Convention. But he wasn't joking! It occurred to me that our beloved and respected conductor was about to become a human tennis ball, being volleyed back and forth for reasons of political persuasion and popularity. A few years ago, I saw Mehta on TV being honored by the same President Bush at the Kennedy Center, and could have sworn I overheard him this time saying, "Let's not put Zubie in the middle," and Mehta responding under his breath that he was now a Republican. He was accompanied by a new wife, who, I understand, was a "roadie," and is a lovely woman. Apparently, the Clintons were fair-weather friends.

Mehta also survived some low-level scandals in Israel, due to his insistence on performing, in the name of intellectual and artistic freedom, the music of the notorious anti-Semite, Richard Wagner. I saw a clip of an Israeli releasing a cow onstage during a performance, which I, myself, likened to public-relations, until I realized that it might have been meant as retribution or offense, being that he was from a predominantly Hindu country, where cows are sacred. Publicists on both sides of the ocean are still trying to figure out what happened. In a world where entertainers are constantly trying to generate coverage for themselves, this situation was ridiculous. It probably was a bright idea of one of the publicists. The bitter sentiment stemming from Mehta's performance of Wagner's works stirred up more unwanted controversy for my domestic department. We were already under so much undeserved stress, even before the attack.

As a result of the Whitewater scandal, I felt I had to keep my eyes and ears open as if our lives were in jeopardy on a daily basis. In my opinion, the incessant grumbling that goes on in the media that sways public opinion against accuracy and democracy hurts Americans, as well as people all over the world who want us to stand up to totalitarianism. On the other hand, thank goodness, the government cannot always manipulate the media.

Simply, because my life flashed before my eyes at the New York

Philharmonic, I had my eye out for stalkers, deranged fans, and even terrorists. What I want to tell you is that it was no coincidence that I saw
Atta that day in Florida. That is why I saw what others did not see. Most
importantly, I feel that I assess our democratic mindset correctly, and
wanted to educate others on how to recognize when democracy is absent,
and how to protect like-minded people.

Unfortunately, I was familiar with different kinds of criminals. The
day in 2001 when I was driving down Atlantic Avenue in Delray Beach,
the tension I saw in the Arab men ahead of me seemed to be politi-
cally motivated, and not just stemming from being in someone else's
neighborhood.

CHAPTER 3

Rendered Speechless: An Attack

YOU MIGHT WONDER HOW an employee of the New York Philharmonic falls from grace, from working in international entertainment publicity, with one of the most glamorous jobs in the
world, to publishing a book about being an unheard citizen. Tenet was
apologetic for the authorities ignoring my tip and said that I was "the
only sane one amongst us. " This chapter was the most difficult for me
to write because I have tried to blot out the trauma from the event, so I
am writing from memory.

A few days after the Whitewater scandal hit, the New York Philharmonic had so many people hanging around that two different representa-
tives of the NSA came to visit our department. The first one told us that
an attack might be imminent, and so he discussed safety routes with us.
I took him seriously, but other employees shirked him off. The second
National Security agent brought a large black briefcase filled with notes,
and Johns believed that he was the real Carl Bernstein. He started jotting
down notes furiously.

I credit the first National Security agent for saving my life. A
deranged fan got through security and asked Eisenberg, who sat at the
front of the department, for "nude photos of Zubin." At first, I thought it

was a joke, but Eisenberg stayed stern. She also stayed silent. He quickly turned into a monster. Eisenberg apparently had a long white gun hidden but she froze in fear of shooting the general public. I started to scream. Security announced over the intercom that they would be there soon, but they were nowhere to be seen. I screamed loudly enough for other staff members to hear me to prevent them from entering.

It became apparent to me that we were being held hostage. I saw the craziness in the eyes of the intruder, craziness I had never seen before, not even in the eyes of my childhood offenders. I escaped onto the third floor outdoor overpass through a large window while the deranged fan started shooting at me and my co-workers. I zig-zagged to the edge, still under gun-fire. Security on the ground gave the order, "Jump, Jump!" I dangled from the edge of the overpass, still in a state of disbelief after shouting to my co-workers to come follow me.

Memories of having practiced jumping out of a school bus came to me. I bent my knees, prayed, and jumped the few stories. I could not believe that I landed on my feet! I ran to a waiting ambulance. Thayer was screaming that I left them, there alone. I ran to the ambulance parked on the piazza near the New York State Theater as I was aspirating heavily and agreed to go to the hospital, but after that I do not remember anything. All of a sudden, the third floor blasted into a million pieces, and I could have sworn I saw dismembered body parts flying in the air, parts of those who used to be my co-workers.

Prior to the blast, Parker had started fighting off the domestic terrorist after he had shot Eisenberg, and had already started shooting at Parker himself. Security on the ground was shouting that Thayer was being raped, but I am still unsure about the number of assailants. A few onlookers assumed that I might be trying to commit suicide because of an obsession with Mehta, or was just vying for attention. Those conclusions were additionally distressing.

Well, the deranged fan did not get photos of Mehta. Thankfully, Mehta was not on the premises, but was conducting in Germany.

I was worried about my parents who were on vacation. I did not want them to hear about the pipe-bomb incident on television, and think that

I had been killed. Somehow, I returned to my dormitory room at New York University that evening, but my friend and roommate told me that I was "not the same." I was to be forever changed by this incident, and the Media Freeze that followed regarding the attack.

The Secret Service agent who earlier had been handling the Clintons, and was later dishonorably discharged, violated my right to Freedom of Speech and Freedom of the Press by keeping the reporting of the details of this attack almost purely under wraps. The National Security Agency tried to ameliorate the situation by cleaning up and having me go back to work the next day. I was told that the authorities were afraid of copycat crimes. Purportedly, Hillary Clinton was fearful for then-Governor Bill Clinton's safety.

As you can see, brushing terror under the rug does not help. It can have a snowball effect until we have a catastrophe such as the attack on September 11, 2001. More recently, A NSA agent, who appeared as Carl Bernstein on CNN and declared that he could not find Neil Parker, so he could not speak to him. The worst part of this scenario was that it pertains to politicians corrupt enough to instill a Media Freeze on the advice of media strategists.

I was further aggravated when Hillary Clinton acknowledged that she herself has never really been under sniper fire abroad, even though she "fibbed" about it during her campaign.

CHAPTER 4
Royal Encounter

O N OCCASION, NOT EVEN princesses live such charmed lives. When I was about ten years old, my mother decided that I would permanently nip my plumpness in the bud if she sent me to a fat camp called Camp Stanley in upstate New York. Camp Stanley's philosophy included forcing pre-teen girls to exercise. I was among the more fortunate that day when I only had only to be a spectator at a baseball game whose participants and spectators were all female campers.

The pitcher was a young girl who happened to be of Israeli extraction. When she heard one of the spectators rooting for the opposing team, she decided to confront the interruption directly from the pitcher's mound. When I turned my head, I could see that whoever decided to start the shouting match looked like she had the wind knocked out of her.

"Please," I recall shouting loudly but politely, "get back to the game." The other spectator exhaled and breathed a sigh of relief. After the game, during dinner in the cafeteria, she walked up to me to thank me for interjecting on her behalf. She had quite an accent, but made herself understood graciously. The next day she told me that her name was Stephanie. Moreover, her grandfather was king of Saudi Arabia. However, there was a catch. Her father's marriage was not exactly sacred by Saudi standards.

Her mother was a woman of German heritage, and not of original Moslem descent. Apparently, when the king, a Wahabi Islamist, was confronted with public criticism regarding the intermarriage of his son, he decided to placate his critics by issuing a statement that he had sent out a "hit-man" to kill his own family members. I had previously dismissed the coverage of their marriage as purely public relations, and did not believe that a royal Saud would ever marry someone deemed inappropriate by the regent. Stephanie did confide in me that she was genuinely fearful of the fatwa that her grandfather declared on her nuclear family. Her family members were known infidels, and were considered disloyal.

Obviously, she was distressed about the "hit-man" sent out to kill her immediate family. The king had cared more about his populace's impression of him as a good Moslem, a descendant of Mohammed, and someone worthy of leadership.

Stephanie asked me to sit next to her at lunch. She told me about the farm her family owned and about how badly the cows smelled. We talked about her father's intermarriage and her own sexuality. I am sure that her appearance was different too; she was fair-haired but dark-skinned; still a stand-out, amongst all her blue-blooded Saudi Arabian cousins. They were more Semitic in appearance, regardless of which of the king's wives from which they were all descended. The problem was her minions. They were three petite females, who harassed anyone they felt was in any way out of line. They were the reason Stephanie had to end the summer early. It was very easy to see how upset she was from the situation.

I realized that Stephanie must have been living in a world that differed from that of her grandfather, and not just because it was on the other side of the ocean. She implored me not to tell anyone where her family was living, even though they were still multi-millionaires. She wanted to hide the information – not out of shame, but out of fear of her immediate family being killed by the "hit-man." As much as I admired Stephanie's lavish lifestyle, I found my own familial situation much less complicated.

However, and I cannot stress this enough, her security disenchanted everyone around them, and I wondered if her entourage had any connection to terror. Stephanie told me about the different terrorist organizations, and Saudi Arabia's struggle with Syria. Even though I believed Stephanie to be innocent, I thought that minions such as hers or their associates could be dangerous. I heard about terrorism all the time from the media, as well from Israelis whom we knew. It occurred to me that the Saudi royal family members do not do their own dirty work, but entrusts subjects who intimidate others to kill innocent civilians, including members of their own family. This is the reason why I distrust the Saudi Arabian government's promise to round-up terrorists, because, if you recall, Saudi Arabia is a state sponsor of terror, and Osama Bin Laden's father was given multi-billion dollar contracts by the Saudi government. Even by royal standards, loyal minions are not easy to enchant, and billions are not easy to come by.

Her father had hired those petite females. His decision to hire them was indicative of the world he was from; a world that forcefully, and even violently, acts in a manner that indicates that the non-Moslem world has no right to exist. For Stephanie's welfare, I won't condemn them. In fact, when Stephanie spoke about Islam, she called it "A nation, a religion of peace." In reply, I told her, "I wish someone, even you, could prove that to me."

CHAPTER 5

The Complaint

BEFORE I GO ANY further in this book, I want to tell my readers about the complaint that brought me into FBI headquarters in West Palm Beach, Florida. I was at home one day when I heard someone knocking loudly on my door. When I answered the door, I saw someone (whom I presumed to be a police officer) barge into my apartment to discuss an alleged stalking charge. Looking down at the street, I could see that the park ranger had left his car running. He told me to sit down, and I sat on the couch while he stood. My mother came out of the bedroom, startled.

Apparently, he was the park ranger at the local Morikami Museum and Japanese Gardens, where I had made an appointment to talk to the then-director. I had to cancel since I had not been feeling well. Despite the fact that I was a no-show, and only made two phone calls to schedule the appointment in the first place, the park ranger accused me of stalking the director, whose name I will not mention.

The park ranger grabbed the gun in his holster. Needless to say, it was an unusual incident. Finally, he left.

Now compound this interlude with a previous occasion where I was driving in a local parking lot, and an Arab man (now identified as

Mohammed Atta), almost crashed into my vehicle. "It must be my own prejudice," I thought, "He's not really crashing into me." An onlooker, who was a young woman similar to me in age, insisted that I contact the authorities. At first, I am ashamed to tell you, I did not even call. About one week later, I was driving down Atlantic Avenue, when I saw the same man being followed by another Arab man as they turned into the Hamlet Country Club development. In the first man's Pinto hatchback, I could see a large pile of papers, which looked like student papers, with a physics diagram. I recognized that the diagram possibly pertained to physics since I had taken a physics course in college.

I could see the political tension in him, even though I stayed friendly. Staying friendly is actually a good piece of advice because you can get to know as much as possible. It would have been much kinder of me to turn them in and spare their lives, even though they would have been arrested. What I noticed was that the physics diagram was of a large rectangle, but open on the bottom, (as if to signify a building). My thoughts turned to the first World Trade Center attack, this time, by plane. These three incidents became the reason why I walked into FBI headquarters. I would like to tell my critics that I did not merely call the police.

I was greeted by the likenesses of Robert Mueller and George Tenet. When I asked why I was greeted by such important men on the ladder of officialdom, I was told that (their likenesses) are to help the psychology of the victim; so to this day I do not know if it was actually them, or just agents in disguise. The supposed "George Tenet" told me he was expecting a tip, and he asked me why I was there. I told them in detail about the strange park ranger incident, and that I wanted it investigated. Later on in the year, I called the park ranger in question, who blamed his previous behavior on the wife of the museum director. When I called to follow up, I was not sure I was speaking to the same person, or just someone who now wanted to exchange pleasantries.

At the FBI headquarters, I was indeed asked about crime in general, and about terrorism in particular, especially in Delray Beach. That's when I remembered that onlooker's insistence that I report the erratic driving, and I told the agents that I saw the two Arab men drive into the Hamlet Country Club. There was a third agent who tried to help me make it clear to the other two agents how important this tip was, and I repeated myself several times upon his insistence. I told them again to check out the Hamlet Country Club. However, I must add that there really was no reason why they should have ignored my complaint, or tip, especially if they were the ones who had asked me about local potential terrorism. I was not unusual in appearance or behavior.

Despite Congressman Lee Hamilton's repeated inquiries at the 9/11 Hearings, we did not get any answers as to why my tip was not followed through by then-CIA spokesman, George Tenet. The FBI and CIA had two weeks to respond and arrest any of the perpetrators on the ground. Tenet said that they were so busy investigating child molesters that they were overwhelmed. However, it was at that time that President Bush received a briefing that a terror attack by Al Qaeda was imminent.

I really should have been treated more respectfully at FBI headquarters, especially if the agents asked if my father was a Central Intelligence agent.

This problem, in my opinion, started when Jimmy Carter rerouted CIA resources into the Department of Agriculture under the false assumption that Central Intelligence agent's salaries should have been cut, when agents may not even receive actual salaries, but are paid by assignment. This is what happened to my family. My father died from a heart attack stemming from kidney failure at the age of fifty-nine. He was a dentist in the private sector, who was forced to retire in his fifties, even though he was not a dentist on assignment. Carter did not even guess accurately how the CIA agents are even paid, yet he did so much damage because foolish people accepted his blame of the country's troubles on the CIA budget, and its possible hidden riches.

Publicly elected officials should work with the CIA, and not against it. They should not inform the public through the media that the CIA is not serving the best interest of our country, which I include standing up to totalitarianism as best we can. Lack of support also leaves the general public wondering why the government is so disorganized. It is highly demoralizing to the agents who sacrifice everything. Also, the CIA should be policing the publicly elected officials, and not the other way around. Carter really wronged us. What would he suggest in place of earning a living? Treason? A lack of resources for the CIA results in a lack of morale for the United States, and for capitalism. As well, such a lack provides opportunities for all our enemies. A lack of resources in protecting our country generates disasters in if we are not prepared for emergencies. It did not help that Carter rerouted billions into Food Stamps, perhaps even into his own till, by being in an agricultural business - the peanut industry.

I do not know how much, if anything, Carter earned from this lack of foresight, but for argument's sake, I will accuse him. Of course, my heart goes out to hungry Americans. However, let's not allow everyone in the country to suffer for the needs of fewer people. Is it a choice of lives over hungry bellies? It is very possible.

Many people are under the false assumption that CIA agents are wealthy, relaxed people and part of an ethnic "majority." In reality, Delray Beach is a decidedly multicultural, middle- class place, with a lot of nice people, and many of them are not CIA agents. I do not recommend the service to anyone. I do not want to see anyone suffer the way that we suffered. An agent's life is filled with secrets and sacrifice.

I remember how we clenched our teeth when my father faced permanent incarceration abroad. I saw how he was ready to commit suicide instead of talking about his assignment. I know about being pushed to the limit of human endurance and showing uncompromising loyalty in the face of corrupt politicians. Dare I include the de facto mistreatment and inequality of minorities of all kinds who are propelled to the four corners of the earth for the sake of freedom and democracy? These are the reasons why I find Carter's actions so repulsive. Please understand me that it is because I want to hold the mantle as high as possible that I criticize him so intensely. Bush, despite his CIA background, did nothing to help the situation before 9/11 hit.

A few years after 9/11, when I saw a protest on TV taking place outside a college CIA recruitment office on a college campus, I silently applauded them. Surprised? Please don't be. We cannot afford to pay the selfless individuals we already have, whom I think of as the best and the brightest. It would be unethical to recruit more cannon-fodder. I don't recommend it. In my opinion, that protester should run for office. His honesty is refreshing. I heard General Michael Hayden say that the CIA is becoming mechanized, and frankly, I do believe him.

Firstly, Carter abandoned us by cutting our resources. Secondly, he betrayed the wheels that put democracy in motion by surrendering to proponents of Middle East dictatorships by rewarding terrorism in dividing Israel (Canaan) into ethnic, artificial divisions, and then he complained that there was apartheid by blaming the Israelis. In reality, the Israelis were the only ones who were giving up anything, namely, their country.

Being the daughter of a CIA operative, and a descendant of Canaanite royalty, I became a very dissatisfied citizen. If Carter thinks there is apartheid, which is an outright inflammatory description in itself, and incites American unrest, he only has himself to blame. He was one of the promulgators of a two-state solution. We should take proper steps to strengthen all our allies and help people all over the world who side with democracy and peaceful multiculturalism. Certainly, we should not forge ties with Hamas, or any terrorist group.

I remember my great-aunt Selma in Israel telling me how she had to go to my cousin's school to search for bombs because the parents would take turns searching. My older cousin serves in the military three months per year and will continue until he is in his fifties. If Carter does not befriend people like me and my nuclear and extended family, who does he befriend? Shouldn't he be on our side?

In fact, Carter showed gross discrimination to CIA agents dispatched to foreign countries. When they got home, they received nothing to help feed their own families. I do not ask for wealth, but only for fairness. If agents are expected to go to the four corners of the earth to face a possible life in prison, I think that they should be shown compassion and, compensation. Carter started the blame game between the government and the CIA. In hindsight, we can see who made the wrong decisions.

Carter blamed the country's ills on the CIA budget during the start of the recession in the 1980's. But later, when the cuts were made, our foreign policies only got worse, until we were left unprepared for two World Trade Center attacks. What we need is a president with judiciousness, and a CIA chief who is not afraid to be a shameless advocate for American objectives, as well as the welfare of his, or her, own employees. Advocating is something that Tenet failed to do.

In fact, Tenet failed to do a lot. When complaining about constraints to CIA activities before 9/11, Tenet, in his book, *At the Center of the Storm: My Years at the CIA*, stated that then-Attorney General Janet Reno would "view an attempt simply to kill Osama Bin Laden as illegal" (page 110), and that airline manifests could not be viewed by the CIA due to privacy issues. Instead of commandeering the NSA, as many Americans would have expected, he blamed others when he wrote that the NSC was not effective.

He discussed the Iraqi-Al Qaeda connection by telling his readers that since the 1990's Al Qaeda had been looking for weapons of mass destruction (WMD). In regard to the terrorism in the Middle East, he wrote that "there was no doubt that Saddam was making large donations to the families of suicide bombers and was known to be harboring several prominent terrorists, including Abu Nidal" (page 346). He also states that Hussein had given refuge to another terrorist who was still being sought for the first WTC bombing.

This indicates to me that our elected politicians are putting different terrorist groups on different levels, depending on how much money that can contribute to a foundation, or how friendly a phony face that can put on their coverage. In my opinion, groups that use funding from totalitarian governments to unleash terrorism on all different kinds of people should really be treated on the same level by the virtue of their tactics.

Tenet did honestly admit that the Middle East is more unstable now than before our "peace" process. He comes to an easy conclusion that Arafat had presented the Palestinian people with violence as an answer to their situation. Due to the increase in violence, more extremism was created, which was an actual obstacle to peace, especially in the view of the Israelis.

Let me reiterate that September 11, 2001 was not the first time that the Department of Justice was ineffective after-the-fact. In 1990, right-wing

Israeli politician Rabbi Meir Kahane was killed in New York by an Egyptian-born assassin. The assassin was eventually arrested and charged, but was only convicted of minor crime charges. Only years later, did Americans learn that the same assassin did have ties to the first WTC bombing, a subject which can now be more easily researched on the Internet.

Tipsters were practically ignored, even if we had told the authorities that these possible terrorists were dangerous. If you believe that it is the policy of the United States government to show compassion to terrorist groups, including Hamas, at whatever price or profit, you are taking the free world in the wrong direction. I also include the formation of an artificial Palestinian state in Israel in this undemocratic sympathy.

CHAPTER 6

Learning the Lesson

I T WAS DUE to the false belief that the messengers of Arab dictatorships could be our friends that we missed the message that terrorists
could be, and are, dangerous. We received the message both loud
and clear on September 11, 2001. Because the CIA kept secretive about
its objectives in general, Carter took advantage of his ability to have a
presumptive photo opportunity, such as the Arafat handshake. This situation misled the American public into thinking that a probable peace
had been achieved, when in reality terrorist groups operated their business as usual, or worse, such as we saw on 9/11. The reason why I saw
what others did not see was because I was a crime victim and a public
affairs specialist. These experiences made me aware of how coverage and
photo opportunities could keep a manipulative Arab dictator in power
in his own country. This personal situation put me on high alert. Then
I saw the two men passing through Delray Beach, Florida.

Thus, I can inform you that 9/11 happened for the following reasons.
Firstly, the justice system is a failure, and a repeal of the Statute of Limitations is imperative so that citizens on the grass-roots level can pursue
justice. Both the Immigration and Naturalization Service, should have
arrested or questioned the terrorists, and the FBI should have expedited a

warrant for their arrest. In short, the terrorists should have been arrested prior to 9/11 on the ground. Actually, it would have been more effective for the CIA and FBI to have looked into what was going on here at home, not abroad. Secondly, the media sometimes assists the misidentification of our ubermoth by covering unusual topics such as prisoner abuse. Of course, I spite the politicians who failed us through misrepresentation and even corruption. This happens when the president and/or senators do not behave in a manner that is conducive to the welfare of our nation as a whole. Even if they do not fully agree with actions that must be taken in order to protect the United States, they must recognize domestic security as their only priority. A foreign policy other than this one is not acceptable. Clinton's Media Freeze resulted in a lack of preparedness to deal with domestic terror, Carter's cutting of resources brought on an emergency, and Bush's lack of action resulted in an additional attack on 9/11.

Also, it seemed to me that during the 9/11 Hearings, Tenet showed how rigid and outdated the CIA hierarchy had become prior to 9/11. In fact, the "Tenet" that I dealt with was rather dismissive. Sadly, we had to start a war in Iraq based on potential WMD, when all it should have taken was that Saddam Hussein had sent an assassin to kill George H. Bush when he was still head of the CIA. Evidence of such an assassin should have been just cause in itself to take action. Lastly, imperfect intelligence is a sure sign that improvements must be made. Most important, the way the system was set up made it possible for American politicians not only to police one another, but stay off the hook for corrupt, or even malicious decisions and acts, regarding the Statute of Limitations. Let's not forget the failure of members of both parties to prevent and prosecute 9/11. The American public truly suffered as neither party held itself, or the other, accountable.

Unfortunately, no country, not even ours, is immune from totalitarianism. The government invariably, and inevitably, shapes its people. Tyrants love when peace-loving people can keep waiting. Recall that Adolf Hitler was able to annex Czechoslovakia, while King George of England thought that Hitler was still a reasonable chap. That thinking changed when Hitler bombarded Britain itself.

CHAPTER 7

Whitewatergate vs. Casketgate

YOU MIGHT THINK THAT because I worked for the New York Philharmonic under Zubin Mehta, I would try to take every opportunity of buttress the Clintons. Nothing could be further from the truth. I blame the Media Freeze which was requested by the Clinton camp and allowed by the Secret Service, to be part and parcel of my feelings of delusion. I consider myself a centrist, and I tell everyone who asks that whoever can give me the most benefits for the least responsibilities is the winner in my book.

The Secret Service told the press almost nothing. I could almost call this incident Whitewatergate because it silenced criticism of the Clintons-criticism that we should have heard before the elections. Also, in the aftermath, they scrambled to step out of bounds to overcome feelings of powerlessness. This was similar to what Nixon did with the issue of eavesdropping in the Watergate scandal. Both actions are incompatible with democracy

You possibly could be a proponent of the Clintons and their policies, such as I was before these incidents. But let me tell you why a Media Freeze is so incredibly dangerous from the right, as well as the left. George Bush was caught recoiling upon hearing that a journalist was taking photographs of flag-covered caskets coming home from Iraq, and I am glad that he hesitated, and did allow the photos to be published. If the president does not allow those photographs to be shown, he prevents us from knowing about the number of casualties. Also, the press could be "frozen" from revealing statistics or releasing coverage of any carnage.

It is not my intention to frighten you, but let me take the possibilities of a Media Freeze a few steps further. Let's imagine that a senator was actually shot, and a Media Freeze, or even a lull, was "indicated." Shouldn't the rest of Congress and the president be warned as soon as possible? What if the shooting was not an isolated case and the Secret Service becomes stressed and was low on personnel? A Media Freeze could play a role in assisting wiping out our democratic institutions. Most importantly, don't the voters have a right to know when a politician becomes incapacitated or there is a security failure? When I heard that the CIA had taken over the role of the Secret Service, I was glad to see that the government was taking a step in the right direction. The justice system has no right to gloss over its own failures, including 9/11. My only other request is that the Supreme Court should render a Media Freeze unconstitutional, even if such a freeze was allowed earlier by the (failed) NSA. A Media Freeze is a violation of Freedom of Speech, as well as a violation of Freedom of the Press. We do not know of any other events that have been "frozen," and short of a Supreme Court case, we won't know. Therefore, the NSA will not be held accountable, even for its disasters.

CHAPTER 8

The National Security Agency and Carl Bernstein

THIS CHAPTER WAS ORIGINALLY written on Thursday, May 28, 2009. As of this date, I am going to tell the general public about my brief encounters with noted Watergate journalist Carl Bernstein, or whoever is posing as Carl Bernstein, on the off-chance that you might accuse either one of us of being self-serving. It is unfair to describe Bernstein as self-serving when he promotes his books and criticism of Hillary Clinton, or describe me that way, saying that I have my own agenda. I have always denied any jealousy over name-sharing as the reason behind my fault-finding. I believe that Bernstein and I are both right to find fault with her.

Last year, "Deep Throat," Bernstein's Watergate informant, was identified as a former FBI chief. All kinds of information and photos are generated about Bernstein on the Internet, including that he has a husband named Carlos. Perhaps he has an alter-ego, or maybe a Latin Romeo. I was wondering about the identity of "Deep Throat" myself.

The Indian gray-man from the New York Philharmonic had even associated the way in which Bernstein was admiring me with the way the Whitewater scandal was generated. It linked with Watergate to become

"Whitewatergate." It wasn't true. I think that the Republican Party in Arkansas was able to dig up dirt on the Clintons, and the bigger newswires picked it up. It was unfortunate that Mehta was involved.

I hate to raise the subject of Bernstein's encounters with the law, but I never brought the statutory rape charges. My parents did not bring any criminal charges, otherwise they would have mentioned it to me. I was as surprised as anyone else that he was brought into a police station, and apparently spent the night in jail. I was shocked when I heard about it on television, especially as my name was mentioned.

He even wrote an article in Vanity Fair about journalists who were affiliated with the CIA. Apparently, he had some criticism of them even though his best breaks and sources were actually from government sycophants themselves. Bernstein is now actually in a precarious situation as a critical journalist working at CNN where there is no shortage of Clinton supporters working as journalists.

The first time I met him I was only sixteen, and he did not behave inappropriately, even though he gave me a compliment that he wanted to see me when I got older. It distressed his then-wife, writer Nora Ephron. I was eighteen the second time I met Bernstein at a lecture in New York City, when I was contemplating becoming a journalist. His assistant was a classmate, and we agreed to share a cab home. Bernstein decided to share our cab, too. The cab was freezing cold. I began to shiver and Bernstein was kind enough to oblige me by holding my hand. Perhaps that's when the chemistry started, and he told me to take the tour of ABC, which I could not.

The next time I saw him, I was fighting off a mugger. I almost spited him for not doing anything, when his security appeared and came to help me. He then showed up at my dormitory to tell me that his niece, Rachel, was thinking about attending New York University. Even though I did not allow Bernstein into my room, Rachel and I became fast friends until she soon transferred. After she faced an attack of her own, she wanted a less stressful situation. She didn't leave New York University, however, without telling me that her uncle had slept with two of her friends.

Rachel visited my house in Old Bethpage once or twice, with her dad, and Bernstein. On their first visit, Bernstein quickly decided to be inappropriate by touching my right breast, even though he was a stranger, and this impulsive action was in front of his niece. That is the time that the NSA became involved, but I do not know if that is due to Bernstein's own concern with security, or my father's secret occupation. However, I believe that the way the NSA overreacted, and the subsequent deletion of Bernstein from the media itself turned him into a protagonist.

A few years later, and after his divorce, I bumped into Bernstein on the street near the New York Coliseum with his then-girlfriend Christine. He asked me if he should marry her, and if I thought it would work out. I told him what I thought. I said that they would be together for many years but it would not work out. She took me to be some kind of rotten kid. He visited the New York Philharmonic, and we leg-wrestled in the Helen Huntington Hull room, where there was a bed. Parker, my supervisor, demanded that I get back to work, and warned me that the CIA would use me for sexual tactics because they did not know how I perked Bernstein's interest. That warning would instill fear in most nineteen-year-old interns. Johns started to complain that things were turning "Potemkin" as if we were living in a Communist-style, artificially created travel village. I felt like I was living inside a touristy snow-globe, looking from the inside-out. Bernstein and I may have experienced quite a bit of personal chemistry, but fear, controversy, and careerism kept me from leaving the premises.

On television, I saw Bernstein on television playing the guitar in Brazil singing about a girl he was in love with from the New York Philharmonic. Then, I saw him on television leave Christine at the altar at a small Vatican wedding. (I didn't know that plump princesses were in such short supply). In the nineties, I bumped into him at a Florida restaurant while he was dining with one of my former New York University professors. When he saw me with my mother and aunt, he started to ask us basic questions. My professor did not like it very much, and left their date early, despite my insistence that their lack of togetherness was not my fault.

The next time I saw him, he was on CNN, almost weeping when he saw that I was the 9/11 "Tipster." He said, "Sweetheart, I never forgot you." Christine accused me of adultery, which was not true. Not even emotional adultery. Finally, I think they did break up. I bumped into Carl with Rachel, and his two charming sons. His mother later told me that Bernstein "wanted it to be." She was extremely polite, and hearing of my mother's illness, she promised me her homemade cheesecake.

The only situation I really did not like was when my personal medical history and perfume were discussed by either the NSA agent, or Carl Bernstein, on CNN. CNN did report, previously, that another tipster was being investigated in California, but I think that he just called the police, and did not go to the FBI.

I want to clarify anyone's notion that I am constantly contacting the authorities, whether it is about statutory rape charges, or potential terrorism. I would like only to encourage the authorities to take our citizenry seriously when they have complaints that bring them into the station, regardless of their station in life or disability.

I need to add that despite my gratitude to the NSA for saving my life at the New York Philharmonic, I abhorred the phony Bernstein for both personal and political reasons.

CHAPTER 9
Gaps in Judgment

I AM AT A loss as to why the authorities did not follow through on my tip about the Hamlet Country Club, which was the development where Atta lived; but my disappointment in them is still better than the grief of the victims of 9/11 and the two wars that were yet to follow. I think that there may have been an official assumption that because the elder Bush had been head of the CIA, and his son had soon followed him into the Presidential office, that any oversights or gaps in domestic security and foreign policy would somehow magically disappear.

George Tenet, at the 9/11 Hearings, stated that it was because other crimes were being investigated that the CIA missed the World Trade Center plot. Later he went on to raise the issue of my mental health, but stated that I was "the only sane one amongst us." Still, I understood that he was just a fall-guy. He was a messenger, whom one still must not shoot, even though he tendered his resignation to make everyone feel better, as if the worst was behind us.

The only participant in the 9/11 Hearings who showed any intelligence and bravery, was Congressman Lee Hamilton. I was tempted to turn off the television when the same questions and answers were repeated over and over again with slight variations. I listened on while Tenet wore out the congressmen, and even though I do not hate Tenet, I will not forgive him for not giving America more honest and direct answers. It also does not help when you see American society, as I do, riddled with crime that is so out of control that potential terrorism is not even investigated!

Indeed, I had become familiar with the possibility of terrorism from my trips to Israel, and my internship at the New York Philharmonic, where suspicious individuals often cased the premises. Shockingly, I believe that the FBI in West Palm Beach thought that the residents of Delray Beach could just handle things on their own, as if little old ladies always carry a pair of handcuffs. I, myself, do not even know if Delray Beach was home to more than people like Granny Bush. What I do know is that there are a lot of grannies in Delray Beach. It would not surprise me if any of those grannies, or grandpas, scared off Al Qaeda from Delray Beach proper.

We all have a right to safety. Hayden, who had previously been head of the Federal Aviation Administration, has always had a good reputation. The new chief perhaps had less experience and thought less security was necessary. Federal Aviation Administration problems, unfortunately, were the last chapter, not the first, in the 9/11 saga. The next-to-last chapter is the Immigration and Naturalization Service. I do not have to belabor the point that one in ten residents is in the country illegally, so I've heard on television. For this reason, I think that the Virtual Wall should be approved. Lastly, and sadly, the local authorities had the chance to discover this plot and missed it.

I do not know if the terrorists hastened their plan for 9/11 as the federal authorities gained more domestic and foreign information, and they became fearful of being arrested, but it certainly would be interesting to know. All I know is that the FBI in West Palm Beach failed us in not arresting the perpetrators. If they did, they could have taken the opportunity to foil their conspiracy.

Perhaps if I had been living a life of privilege, the agents at FBI headquarters would have taken me more seriously, but unfortunately, my mother is a dialysis patient, and so was my father. Even though we are a bright family, we are relatively unlucky in the health and wealth category.

I have been asked why I am not working for, and at, the New York Phil-harmonic, and frankly, I do not want to be in public-relations, and do not relish taking my life in my hands.

The Whitewater scandal affected the personalities of my whole department, where they were not the pleasant individuals they used to be, after dealing with all the stress and stalkers. Even though I was asked to continue my internship the next semester, I decided against it. Often, the perception of the entertainment industry and reality are quite different. That conclusion can also pertain to public people, and especially politi-cians: perception is not reality.

CHAPTER 10

A Funny Situation

WALKED INTO THE Department of Vocational Rehabilitation for my
appointment. The previous year I had met a CIA medic at a syna-
gogue, and all he talked about was how he loved physical challenges
showing his readiness for different assignments. He had told me that
he worked for the Department of Vocational Rehabilitation. My friend
Margie, who has a nervous problem, told me a few months later that
he was assigned to her, and was even nice enough to drive her to a few
interviews! In any case, the man who was assigned to my case locally
was a family man, with a photo of his wife and children on his desk.
He later became exasperated when I told him that I could not show up
to his 8:30 a.m. workshop. He told me that he worked very hard to orga-
nize it. He also asked me my opinion on whether his saving of plastic
packaging was considered "normal." I told him that I did not know,
even though I did not think it was, except perhaps to recycle. Then the
bombshell hit.

He told me that he himself was a CIA agent. We started to talk about
Communism in the former Soviet Union. I asked why George Bush said
that Communism fell by itself. He said that it was due to sexual tactics
by the Soviets. Such tactics, I learned, exploits the predator more than the

prey. All I know is that the warning I had received from my New York Philharmonic supervisor, Neil Parker, was taken in good faith, and I wanted to be spared being victim or a perpetrator.

It was unspoken by the Department of Vocational Rehabilitation specialist that it was the resentment by their own agents that caused Communism to fail. That is not to say that Capitalism could not fall the same way. I believe that leaning on agents so heavily and demanding that sexual tactics be used are approaches that are dangerous. We must also consider the question of such behavior as being inherently unethical. In fact, a probable cause of 9/11 is that the elected government demanded too much of the CIA and its employees. The demands included performance without resources for themselves, their jobs, and their families. To use a colloquialism, if you put garbage in, you get garbage out.

Modern totalitarian governments are noted for their Potemkin villages and sexual tactics. Importantly, Communist-style sexual tactics should have no place in the behavior of any free nation. That is why I am distrustful of gratuitous affection by foreign officials. There is a spectrum of tactics, from bad to worse, which must be rejected if we want to breathe just a little in the free world. That is why a country should stay upstanding in its tactics. I do not like Big Brother in Israel, but I truly hate the terrorist tactics of other governmental entities in the Middle East.

We can do the world a world of good if we understand that no country is exempt from dictatorship, not even the United States. In extreme cases, the victims themselves are blamed for the violence. The Arab nations who have dictatorships have been "blessed" with generations of aggressive Islamist leaders who do not think twice about using their own populace for their own objectives. Thus, they generate suicide bombers to intimidate domestic and foreign populations after they lose consecutive wars with Israel. If we push Israel to the brink with criticism, and arguments for "peace," I am afraid that we will weaken our own objectives. The other possibility is religious extremism. We may have to tell both the Palestinians and the Israelis that they have to live in the gray, knowing that is not what they want to hear.

With all the terrorism of the Palestinian splinter groups, I think that it would be in the best interest of the United States to keep them as weak as possible. At the same time, I would be for a democratic, and peaceful, Palestinian homeland along its ancient borders with Canaan, with a capital at Aleppo, the gravesite of Palestinian conqueror, Suleiman. We should have true boundaries and only reward peace, and not continuous terror. There are large Palestinian populations in several other countries, not just in Israel. If a Palestinian state were to be established, thousands, if not millions of unwanted people would rush Israel. You and I both know that the terror groups would be hell-bent on violence. That violence would do damage to the only democratic state in the Middle East. By rewarding terror with the promise to the Palestinians of land and resources from Israel, our politicians have only created a snowball effect until it hit New York, the Pentagon, and Pennsylvania. This division policy also rings of a divide and conquer policy that the British Empire purportedly used and which generated extreme violence.

CHAPTER 11

Will the Real Instigator Please Stand Up?

I T IS WRONG TO conclude that all the Middle East's problems are caused by Israel. OPEC would charge us as much as possible for oil, with or without, the State of Israel; it is just human nature, and greed. Egypt now holds the Sinai, and Gaza is populated by Palestinians. I believe that all people want to live free from atrocities, and free in their own land, if not their own indigenous nation. It is another outrage when American policies are an obstacle to that sovereignty. It rings back to the injustices that were inflicted on the American Indians and "imported" Africans. It can happen again, and it is happening right now.

However, a President such as Andrew Jackson, who was controversial, was also popular because he understood that the need for political asylum of his own population met the expression of indigenous rights. He was a shameless advocate for his own population after suffering at the hands of the British Empire. Now, we are fighting for both; against an Islamist Empire, and for indigenous, human rights for Canaanites/Israelis. I want whoever is in office to recognize the truth. Israel has been fighting the Islamist Empire for decades, and it is time that the American government criticizes, if not fights, the actually guilty parties. This is more important than talking about money with Hamas, as Carter did, or accepting millions for their foundation, such as the Clintons did from the Saudi Arabian royal family. Obviously, the Arab media prohibits any back-talk, and the Western media seems to cower, and no recent president has had the bravery to criticize the destruction of a democracy in the Middle East as Israel is pressed to settle more demands.

It seems that our government is more afraid of left-wing Socialism or Communism in Israel than Arab aggression, which is a big mistake. As you know, Israel is filled with Refuseniks, people who suffered to leave the former Soviet Union, and it's doubtful that they want to relive that type of Soviet government in their new land. Our politicians, except for President Obama, have missed one great photo opportunity. They should have posed with Refuseniks to acknowledge them on their trips to Israel. I do not blame them for the fall of Communism, but I do feel that Refuseniks deserve to be acknowledged, and befriended.

In addition, the policy of insisting on a Palestinian state in Israel and the former British occupation of Palestine/Israel could generate the need for another apology, and an assurance that we do not really mean to threaten Israel's autonomy. Secretary of State Clinton, unfortunately, has the habit of leaving the messes behind her, and blaming other people. I am also referring to the Media Freeze, the right-wing conspiracy theory, the Oklahoma bombing, and two World Trade Center attacks including 9/11. Yet, she brilliantly deflects criticism as if ever blaming her, must be the fault of the right-wing. President Obama's saving grace was that he was able to get the Democratic nomination, and agrees that the capital of a Palestinian country should be Aleppo.

In the end, the NSA gave us little security, and the decision to allow the Media Freeze possibly snowballed into 9/11. In addition, voices of criticism were also stifled in the name of progressive politics, which, in turn, victimized thousands of innocent average Americans. In my opinion the Media Freeze was one of the worst decisions ever made of behalf of this country. It is no coincidence that these politicians were in power when 9/11 hit the rest of America, as it had hit me already, just not as forcefully.

CHAPTER 12

My Speech

WHEN I SAW THE 9/11 families gather at Ground Zero, I started to think of a speech to them, in order to help them through their ordeal. If I had to stand before the families of the victims of 9/11 and uplift them to a point where they could be comforted, I would say that we received a message. The message is that we cannot tolerate any violation of our rights, namely, Freedom of Speech, as well as the Freedom of the Press. The Media Freeze goes against our grain. I was affected, and the public and authorities were left unprepared. The FBI did not know what a great threat domestic terror was, since the New York Philharmonic attack went largely unreported. In actuality, the Clintons' Media Freeze, and Carter's additional friendliness toward terrorists and their associates lethally obfuscated the message that our freedom and security was in jeopardy.

We should also not tolerate when our own government assumes the identities of journalists, including the NSA agent posing as Carl Bernstein. In my speech, I would say that the needed rejuvenation of these freedoms is the reason the New York Philharmonic staff and the victims of 9/11 suffered. We can honor them by fighting the circumstances that let these catastrophes happen. Let me comfort the survivors with the thought that if you join me in entrenching our Freedom of Speech, demand a lack of governmental corruption, and even repeal the Statute of Limitations, we can all sleep better by knowing that we will not let the 9/11 victims die in vain. My intention is not only to improve the justice system, but also hold the government accountable for the lack of justice in this country.

CHAPTER 13
On High Alert

ORMER PRESIDENT JIMMY CARTER blamed many of the country's ills on the CIA budget. But afterwards, when the budget cuts were made, our foreign policies only got worse to the point that we were unprepared for two World Trade Center attacks. As operations are supposed to become more technologically advanced, I expect them to also become more expensive, which should tempt the powers that be to propel more potential employees to stay in the private sector, and not recruit more people. I hate to say it, but I feel that my family was treated with discrimination, especially regarding the attack at the New York Philharmonic and the little direction in helping us.

The fact that the Clintons wanted to brush the coverage of the attack under the rug did not help either. The Secret Service agent who decided to host his own press conference, and was only but recently discharged, should not have taken the microphone, but should have let the media take its natural course in covering events, including speaking to the police and witnesses. Such a power grab really is not compatible with democracy. Presidents should offer a foreign policy that protects our citizens, not one that rewards terrorism, or any aggression, especially for profit.

In fact, the national security that was offered was more like national insecurity. The Media Freeze was an undemocratic request that hurts America's infrastructure. Knowing that it takes an Act of Congress to do almost anything, we need to be ready for possible, even probable, nuclear terrorism. I cannot accept that Mrs. Clinton received twenty million dollars from the Saudi royal government for her foundation, a government that enabled the Bin Ladens in the first place. The Saudi Arabian government is a state sponsor of terror, including the televising of telethons for terrorists and suicide bombers. Silence and distraction are the reasons how the American public was left uneducated about terrorists in our midst. Saudi Arabia, Syria, and Iran all use terrorism as unofficial tactics to manipulate foreign and domestic populaces into ultimate compliance. George W. Bush even cited Iraq as a haven for terrorists, and despite having splinter groups, terrorists really have only one objective, and that is control.

I would have chosen Iraq as a tertiary target as far as declaring war is concerned, but Bush had a personal and professional vendetta against Hussein. Hussein sent an assassin to kill his father, who had been head of the CIA. Bush did say that Iraq is central in geographical location to the Arab Islamist Empire, and it is possible that he chose Iraq for that reason, but I do not believe it. I might have been less eager to find Bin Laden, (but not to release his family), and more inclined to punish governments that sponsor terror and enable Al Qaeda in the first place. I do believe that the Saudi Arabian "reeducation camps" are deceitful attempts to round up terrorists. I think that an Islamist is more likely to follow, than rebel against, the descendants of Mohammed that are in power in the Arab world.

My best tip is that, if you want to catch a terrorist, think like a terrorist. You want a photo opportunity to please your dictator back home, where there is not a free press, at all. That is what came to my mind while I was driving down Atlantic Avenue and saw two of the terrorists of the disaster of 9/11. There could even be collusion between Bin Laden, and other governments that sponsor terror. Those types of governments want to stay in control of their own population by means of intimidation.

What I saw in that other driver, now identified as Mohammed Atta, was someone who was inspired to act for an Arab photo opportunity, not in the United States, but back home, for power's sake. I saw the political and physical tension that he was trying to hide. He was a minion, similar to Stephanie's entourage, but on full throttle. Unless we all want to become minions of our own government, we must hold on to our blessed freedoms for all they are worth, whether we are to the left, or to the right on the political spectrum..

President Barack Obama has recently called the option of a Palestinian state in Israel as "unsustainable." This does not surprise me. With all of the terrorism of the Palestinian splinter groups, I think that it would be in America's best interest to keep them as weak as possible, knowing that the terrorist groups may not emanate from the Palestinian people, but do affect them greatly. I think that the answer, as implausible as it may sound, would be for a democratic and peaceful, Palestinian ancestral homeland along its ancient border with Canaan, with its capital at Aleppo, the gravesite of Palestinian conqueror, Suleiman. Europe has faced such a situation before, with Aquitaine, or territories between France and Germany that were the scene of gross bloodshed. Countries are not known to give up their ancestral lands without outright war.

We should have true boundaries and only reward peace, and not continuous terror. By rewarding terror, our politicians only created a snowball effect until it hit the United States.

CHAPTER 14
Neda

THE ONLY FAVOR FOR which I can actually thank George Tenet is mentioning that I am a descendant of Canaanite royalty, and that is for almost purely social reasons. Many of you, I am sure, were raised with the notion that only one human entity can be the Messiah. However, culturally I have been raised with the ancient Canaanite concept that the idea of a messiah is dichotomous. The first meaning is being a messiah through deliverance, and the second, is through suffering. In fact, I have heard the exclamation that a messiah is born in every generation, a supposition that propelled me into action. My mother also had this type of praise for Martin Luther King when he was assassinated.

Allow me to describe messianic political suffering in an individual who stands up to totalitarianism at the expense of their own life, and a young Iranian music student named Neda comes to my mind, who was shot in the head from a rooftop while participating in a protest against a dictator, Mahmoud Ahmadinejhad, who denies the Holocaust, continues to profligate nuclear war against the demands of the whole world, and even cuts off communication among his own citizens. Even though Neda did not carry her own testament the way Jesus did, her message is certainly clear. Her suffering for political change in Iran is what is going to deliver not only her own country, but also the Middle East, and maybe the rest of the world as well. It is her sacrifice that makes our lives easier, and honors innocent people, such as Holocaust victims who have lost their lives at the hands of other dictators.

I am sure that you have seen the commercial, "Come to Israel, come stay with friends." Well, I think that song is not completely wrong, but a better observation would be, "Israel, where the West begins." In fact, I have heard television coverage that according to DNA studies, one in four Israelis has a non-Canaanite ancestor. The ancestor could possibly be from Europe, Babylon, Asia, or even Africa. Many Jews who visit Israel come to the casual conclusion that Israel's Western-style democracy is part of the reason why many Palestinians are there, and very much want to stay there. I am of the firm belief that if democracy could be truly exported to the Arab world, and ancestral Palestine in particular, with its capital at Aleppo, both sides, (Canaan/Israel and Palestine) could have a true chance at peace. However, I do not recommend another situation such as the division of Pakistan and India where there was bloodshed. The Palestinians have been living on the land since pre-Christian Romans renamed the land from Israel to Palestrina. Then, after Mohammed, Suleiman, who is buried in Aleppo, annexed the land as part of Palestine. Then, Palestine (not Canaan/Israel), became part of Syria. Other Islamists have caused Palestinians to be dispossessed of their own land. The cause was not Israelis who just want to live in the country of their own ancestors and spiritual brethren. Yet, an entire Islamist onslaught hits the small country of Israel, on the platform of religious and political convenience and cohesiveness. That does not mean that Palestinians living in Israel should not have parity, but it must be with societal understanding that all individuals must function as part of that society, and not in opposition to it.

My family and I refer to ourselves as Canaanite nationalists partly because we want everyone to understand that we are indigenous to our land, just as an Englishman is English, or a Frenchman is French. All Jews, however, are brethren, who may deserve to be a part of the Jewish state due to the sufferings of history, and especially the Holocaust. We do not wish to duress anyone, but seek to propel Canaan as far into the future as possible. Islamist governments that continue to use Palestinians as a pawn in the continuance of totalitarianism and terrorism intimidate their victims to make sure that they can take no part in a true democratic society.

I am forced to comment on our leaders' bad decision-making, which rings of a "divide-and-conquer" approach. This is a tactic that the British Empire was accused of many times. Carter not only cut CIA resources thereby weakening us, but he betrayed me by violating my indigenous rights by caving into the objectives of governments that backed terrorism. Hillary Clinton was worse in that she continued these actions, plus her minions manipulated the media right here in the United States by the use of political consultants as journalists on CNN.

CHAPTER 15

My Statement

PART OF THE reason why I wanted to write *Tipster: A Look at How 9/11 Happened*, is because I felt that I was spited for not coming forward, even though part of my life has been replete with secrets and sacrifice, including my father's "second" career. However, when Tenet started to describe the quagmire of investigation surrounding child molesters from my past as to the reason why he did not send investigators to the Hamlet Country Club, I felt compelled to come forward. "That was my limit," I thought, "I am going to talk," and "I am going to stop suffering for the welfare of my fellow Americans." May I add that this was a difficult decision for me, filled with the fear of possible future humiliation and strong feelings of a betrayal of secrecy?

A few years ago, I went to the courthouse in Delray Beach to discuss many of the crimes perpetrated against me during my childhood, and I was told that no prosecutor would take the cases because it was past the Statute of Limitations. Children cannot testify against their abusers, but when they become adults, the Statute of Limitations has passed. Victims not only are rendered powerless by their abusers, but also victimized again by the justice system itself.

Whether or not the decision to have the Media Freeze snowballed into 9/11 can be a source of political conjecture, but, in my opinion, it was a major contributor, and it was very unfortunate that I was involved. I believe that the authorities, especially in New York, would have become more conscientious of the possibility of the occurrence of terrorism, whether it be perpetrated by a deranged fan in New York, the bombing of innocent civilians in Oklahoma, or eventually, not one, but two World Trade Center catastrophes. The Clintons' need for "personal safety" should have been put into the perspective of the public's need not only for safety, but, paradoxically, national security. It's a tragedy that the NSA had such poor foresight and bad decision-making. Also, the attack at the New York Philharmonic was almost seen as a ploy for sympathy for the Clintons regarding Whitewater, despite the fact that they were not on the premises at the time, and the Media Freeze victimized the hostages for a second round.

Alexander Hamilton stated, "Give me liberty, or give me death." What he meant was that he preferred death to suffering through the atrocities of totalitarianism. I am going to add a meaning to this sentence. Without liberty, there is death, as we discovered on 9/11, after a Media Freeze, and politicians who promulgated the rights of dictator-based terrorist groups over the welfare of its own citizenry.

Even though I never had the luxury of having my own press conference or releasing a public statement to the media right after George Tenet named me as a tipster prior to the occurrence of the September 11 attacks at the 9/11 Hearings, I have always felt the need to come forward, and speak to the people, despite my father's background as a CIA operative, and all the secrets, sacrifice, and restrictions surrounding our lives. I want to ask you for your respect. Silence was actually much more painful than self-validation. It occurred to me immediately that the public deserved to hear from me. My emotions ranged from anger, and fear, to despondency. My despondency lifted, and my forgiveness only started, when my father was named as an operative. However, my father's character was such that he would have never come forward, and many of his colleagues would actually laud him for it. The will of the people actually won when

I was mentioned because it shows that the CIA (Tenet) was, in some way, accountable to the people of the United States who demanded an explanation, and not solely accountable to his failed governmental agency or to any of the politicians to whom he had to answer, whether or not their negligence or corruption were responsible for the attack in the first place. However, the answers should have been much richer in detail, and not so rich in repetition.

Unfortunately, the 9/11 Hearings did not descend into finger-pointing, which is something that I do try to do in my book. I try to show in this book how the actions of a few politicians were responsible for our security failures by trying to bend our system of freedom into something from which they could profit. Our politicians then allowed themselves the corruption of not being held accountable, even during the 9/11 Hearings. This lethal governmental corruption was accompanied by possible manipulation of the media, who often by covered a pro-terrorist format repeatedly, by portraying the Palestinians and terror groups as disadvantaged.

I would have loved to have had a press conference and be the center of attention as the only private citizen who could have prevented 9/11. Silence and insignificance were excruciating for me. Just simple chit-chat does not get us closer to any answers. The reason why television personalities have resorted to these verbal blips is because it has been nearly impossible to blame a few publicly elected politicians (and their failure and corruption) for what happened on 9/11. Just like common criminals, they can take advantage of their own power, and even have a Statute of Limitations. We saw how Democrats policing Democrats, and Republicans policing Republicans, and even each other, failed us. It was sad that the CIA was relatively silent, the NSA was not called forward and even the FBI deferred to the CIA and was able to use Central Intelligence Agency secrecy as a cloak of hiding their failures. In every regard, I was the victim of silence, and the victims of 9/11 were victimized again by governmental silence and a circuitous volley of blame.

Let me say that I am not writing this book for popularity, but for humanity. When I mentioned potential terrorism regarding the Hamlet Country Club during my meeting at FBI headquarters in West Palm

Beach, Florida, the agency had two weeks to apprehend the 9/11 hijackers. It is a symptom of what's wrong. In a failed justice system such as the one we have, it is a lethal blow to allow all law-breakers, including politicians, to operate freely without too much fear of facing consequences. Our system allows a Statute of Limitations that punishes victims seeking justice. It is an uncomfortable place to be, like a wound that needs to be cleaned before it can be allowed to heal.

CHAPTER 16
Conclusion

WE ALL MIGHT HAVE seen 9/11 coming if the media covered how totalitarian governments who sponsor terror manipulate their way into power, and stay there. I knew that a photo opportunity of the World Trade Center, capitalism's jewel, would be valuable to the hostile Islamist governments that seek to prosper from any free nation's difficulties.

If you add more than seven wars between Israel and the Arab countries, I will show you that the only way for peace our way is to stay on high alert to protect our civilians. The two-state solution that is being proposed by our politicians rings back to the failures of Britain and the United Nations to divide the country of my ancestors into Israel and Trans-Jordan. The British Mandate, or Occupation, depending on how you look at it, resulted in both Israeli and Egyptian terrorism against the British, and it was "successful." The British pulled out, even when the rest of the world was being divided into possible "divide and conquer" situations, such as with India and Pakistan; North and South Korea; and East and West Germany.

The almost constant criticism of Israel in the media and the insistence on two-states in Canaan, one which will not be based on democracy, will do nothing to help the situation. I am glad that Israel has a modicum of a multi-cultural population, as I have a few non-Canaanite ancestors myself. I want to stress that ancient Palestine was a separate country from Canaan/Israel. One Diaspora does not deserve another, but the Islamist nations should stop insisting that Palestine has its roots in the Canaanite/Israeli Jewish nation.

Perhaps it was my mindset that caused me to notice the hostility of the two drivers that afternoon on Atlantic Avenue in Delray Beach. If we understand that totalitarian governments do not base their policies on reason, but on power, we can learn how to try to protect ourselves. If we insist on freedom for our own country, and join together, not out of fear, but out of strength, we can make the whole world a better place. Lastly, we can propel that world as far into the future to a safe, democratic place, one that we can all truly call home, no matter where we live, or what, or who, we are.

www.ingramcontent.com/pod-product-compliance
Lightning Source LLC
Chambersburg PA
CBHW060215290526
45789CB00003B/1277